ABSOLUTELY Unforgettable

THE ENTREPRENEUR'S GUIDE
To Creating A Heart-Centered Brand And Standing Out In A Noisy World

STEPHANIE NIVINSKUS

FREE BONUS TRAINING

This book includes links to step-by-step implementation worksheets you can use RIGHT NOW to create your absolutely unforgettable brand.

>>> GET THEM NOW at SizzleForce.com/BookBonus

Absolutely Unforgettable: The Entrepreneurs Guide To Creating A Heart-Centered Brand And Standing Out In A Noisy World

By Stephanie Nivinskus
Copyright ©2018 by Stephanie Nivinskus and SizzleForce, Inc.

ISBN 13: 978-1985837232
ISBN 10: 1985837234

10755 Scripps Poway Parkway #134
San Diego, California 92131

www.SizzleForce.com
PublishMe@SizzleForce.com

DEDICATION

To my husband, Kevin. Because of the way you live and love, my life is better than I ever dreamed it could be. You are and always will be the love of my life. I'm so thankful for you.

And to my children, Joshua, Josiah and Ella. Words are insufficient to describe the depth of my love for you. I'm so honored to be your mom. I love you most.

TABLE OF CONTENTS

Table of Contents

Chapter One

IN THE BEGINNING

/1/

IN THE BEGINNING

Time stops. Or at least it feels like it does. Every single time I enter this store, I am overcome by the way it makes me *feel* when I shop here. Chic. Feminine. Beautiful. And dare I say, valuable?

They say happiness comes in their yellow box and I have to agree. There's something truly magical about the brand they've created—something few can boast of. And it's made them *absolutely unforgettable.*

Kendra Scott has taken her spare bedroom start up to a place most only dream of. Her fashion and lifestyle brand recently earned the coveted title of a unicorn—a private company with a valuation of over $1 billion. Furthermore, she's also been named one of America's richest self-made women by Forbes. And that's just the beginning. There's more than enough evidence that supports she's doing something right with her branding. Something *very right.*

What makes a brand absolutely unforgettable? Considering there is virtually no limit to the amount of information the human brain can retain, why do we forget most of the brands we encounter? And what are Kendra Scott and the rest of the world's most memorable (and profitable) brands doing differently? What is their secret sauce to standing out in this noisy world, and perhaps most importantly, is there any left for the rest of us?

I vote yes. *Absolutely yes.* We just have to uncover it.

What A Brand Is. (And What It Isn't)

Maria Von Trapp said it best. The beginning is indeed a very good place to start. That said, let's follow her lead and explore this idea of how to create an unforgettable brand from the very beginning.

First, we must clearly understand what a brand is and what it is not. Much to the dismay of many graphic designers, a brand is not a logo. A logo is a graphic of a company name and/or symbol that visually represents the promise that company makes to the marketplace.

Think Nike's iconic swoosh. While it conveys a sense of movement and speed and has been used with and without the word Nike next to it, by no means whatsoever does that one graphic image encapsulate the entire Nike brand. The Nike brand is far more than its swoosh. It's the multi-faceted emotional connection the company makes with the marketplace. It's what people say about them in their private conversations. It's their story, promise, core values, personality, position, philosophy, mission, products, service, philanthropic outreach and so much more. Nike's brand is why people choose to buy from them, instead of Reebok, Adidas, Puma or Fila and countless other manufacturers of similar products.

Just like we cannot say the yolk of an egg is an egg in and of itself, we cannot say a logo is a brand. It's just a little part of it. However, that's not to downplay its importance by any means. Logos play a key role in branding. They just don't play the *only* role.

Sometimes, when you run a small business, all of this branding talk can feel like it's way out of your league. Sure Coca Cola, Apple, and Starbucks have invested obscene amounts of money creating and managing their brand, but is it really something the small business owner should even think about?

Yes. Yes. And yes.

The Small Business Administration considers any business with fewer than 500 employees or $7.5 million in annual receipts a small business. It's true. Google it. In 2002 Kendra Scott started her company with some handmade jewelry, her baby strapped to her back and $500. Did she have the elaborate store branding she has now way back then? Of course not. She didn't even have a store at that point. But she still created and managed her brand. And so should you.

Why You Must Create Your Brand

Truth bomb: If you have a business, you have a brand. Either you've taken intentional steps to create your brand or the marketplace has created it for you based on their perception of you. The latter is dangerous. Spend two minutes reading feedback on any review site and you'll very quickly see, the public can be downright brutal. Internet trolls perch themselves on high and mighty branches every day seeking out brands they can destroy as they spew their venom from behind their keyboard.

In many cases, these trolls leave harsh reviews purely for their own sick sense of enjoyment. In some cases, they do it because they're competing with you. And of course sometimes, those nasty reviews are written by people that had a really bad day and a less-than-perfect experience with your brand and just need to vent. In most cases, the really vile reviews are rarely an accurate reflection of the average customer experience.

Several years ago I had a client that owned a restaurant tell me he'd received an outrageous review on Yelp. It said, "I'd rather vomit in my mouth and swallow it than eat anything from this joint."

Frustrated, he contacted Yelp and asked for the review to be removed only to learn they would not remove it. He was told their algorithm could detect legitimate reviews from illegitimate ones and this one was legit.

While it bruised his ego initially and caused him some unnecessary stress, it had no long-term negative impact on his business for one reason and one reason only: his brand. Because he was operating a business that intentionally created and managed its brand, the flaming darts the trolls threw at him were virtually harmless.

Why You Must Manage Your Brand

There are a million reasons why you absolutely must manage your brand. Truth is, it's human nature to gravitate toward what you know, like and trust. The more intentional you are about managing your brand, the more likely you'll witness the positive results of doing so. The benefits of brand management are countless, but here are ten of my favorite:

1. **You will be perceived the way you want to be perceived.**
   Walmart is known as the low-price leader because that's what they aimed for in their branding. Hermes, Prada and Louis Vuitton have done the exact opposite—positioning themselves at the other end of the spectrum.

2. **You will set yourself apart from your competition.**
   Unless you've invented a product no one has ever seen or heard of before, you've got competition. If you want to stand out as the best choice, you have to position yourself accordingly. That's accomplished through branding.

3. **You will be able to command a higher price point.**

   Every day Apple sells computers, iPods, iPhones and more to loyal fans that will pay far more for their products when they could get products with fairly similar capabilities for a fraction of the price. Why? Because they're Apple. And they can. *And so can you.*

4. **You will create an enviable internal culture that attracts top-performers.**

   Want to become a magnet for the best talent in your industry? Create an absolutely unforgettable brand. When you ooze everything your tribe loves, you become irresistible.

5. **You will build brand loyalty that's impossible to buy.**

   You're either an iPhone or Android customer. A Pepsi lover or a Coke lover. A Canon girl or a Nikon girl. But you and the rest of the world know, there's one thing you're NOT—a fan of both. In fact, it's a cardinal sin to favor both. Branding makes people take sides. And more often than not, once fans take a side, they become fierce protectors of it. If someone on the opposing side attacks you, a well-managed brand will have their own tribe of unpaid brand advocates fighting to protect your brand more than you ever could. And those who get the most people on their side always win the game.

6. **You will create marketplace clarity that practically guarantees repeat business.**

   If you own a brick and mortar business and have more than one location, a well-managed brand will assure you that you'll have a similar experience doing business with that brand regardless of which location you visit. Think Starbucks and you've got the right idea. The overall customer experience—from the drink menu to the hip vibe—is identical in every single store. If a customer loves your brand experience, they'll come back again and again.

7. **You will assemble a tribe of raving fans that will do anything to buy what you sell (and will tell their friends to do the same).**

   Want people to wait in a line that circles the block when you release a new product? Eager to see people camp out in front of your place so they're first in line when you open your doors? Well-managed brands see that kind of stuff on a regular basis.

8. **You will create unpaid brand advocates that advertise for you.**

   The world's most unforgettable brands are so lovable their people actually do the advertising for them. They tattoo their logo on their flesh, slap logo stickers all over their car, wave flags in front of their house and become walking billboards as they sport t-shirts with your logo front and center.

9. **You will get the sale (while your competitors watch).**

   While not everyone in your target market is ready to buy as soon as you're ready to sell, they will be ready to buy eventually. Well-managed brands are the first to come to mind when your ideal clients are ready to pull out their wallets. And often the brand they think of first earns the sale.

10. You will connect with your customers at an emotional level.

90% of purchases are based on emotions. Enough said.

Now that we have established the necessity of creating and managing your brand, we are ready to explore the risky business the world's most unforgettable brands know all about.

> ## KEY TAKEAWAYS
>
> - A brand is not a logo. It's the multi-faceted emotional connection a company makes with the marketplace.
> - If you have a business, you have a brand. Either you've taken intentional steps to create your brand or the marketplace has created it for you based on their perception of you.
> - It's human nature to gravitate toward what you know, like and trust.

Chapter Two

RISKY BUSINESS

11

CHAPTER TWO: RISKY BUSINESS

The world's most unforgettable brands all have one thing in common: they take risks. They break rules. They speak out when most are silent. They disrupt. They're bold, passionate and authentic and when you encounter them, you're never left to wonder where they stand.

In my 30's, I represented the brand The Body Shop for five years. During that time, I had the pleasure of talking with Anita Roddick, the founder of the company, on more than one occasion. Always oozing with the perfect blend of passion and recklessness, even the briefest of conversations with Anita were always unforgettable.

Unlike many of my peers, it wasn't her brand that attracted me to her company—it was merely the fact that I'm a glutton for girly girl lotions and potions and she created some of my favorites. But I was the odd duck. Nearly everyone else I knew at the company was drawn to the opportunity because of Anita's fierce stance on animal testing, protecting the environment and what she called "moral leadership."

Long before "being green" was a thing, Anita was unapologetically advocating for her core beliefs through her company and in doing so, building a tribe of fiercely loyal enthusiasts. When the cosmetics industry as a whole was centered on profitability, conventional beauty, and business as usual, Anita put idealism back on the corporate agenda. And it was her radical idealism that was the driving force behind the heart-centered brand she built that stood out in a very noisy world. So much so, that she grew her one little store in London into more than 2,000 locations in 50 countries around the world.

"Well behaved women rarely make history," she said. It was Anita's willingness to misbehave (at a time when a misbehaving woman was frowned upon) that made her brand absolutely unforgettable.

While misbehaving may have worked well for Anita, it doesn't work well for everyone. There's a fine line between misbehaving just enough to shake things up and garner favorable attention and misbehaving in a way that makes you nothing short of repulsive in the marketplace. Few know how to walk that line gracefully like Anita did which is exactly why today's brands must take risks in other ways. The good news? There are plenty of ways to do just that.

GEICO is prime example of a brand that takes big risks in an unconventional way. They've made insurance—perhaps the most boring industry in the world—entertaining. And in doing so have given giants like Allstate and State Farm a serious run for their money.

Although the company has been in business since the 1930's, it was in the early 1990's, when they hired a new chairman named Olza "Tony" Nicely, that the company took a big risk—replacing ho-hum insurance advertisements with the GEICO Gecko®, who—simply put—just didn't belong in an insurance ad. But that's what made it so unforgettable.

It wasn't long before the company then introduced its Cavemen campaign—the one that said geico.com was "so easy even a caveman can do it." The advertisements went viral, and were often said to be *so good*, they were *unskippable*.

Wait…stop.

Car insurance? Geckos? Cavemen? *Seriously?*

Yes, seriously. GEICO's willingness to take bold advertising risks has attracted more than 15 million policy holders. With that kind of profit, you can buy a whole lot of geckos.

When considering brands that take risks, we cannot forget what Dove has done with their "Movement for Self-Esteem" (formerly called "Campaign for Real Beauty") ads. Philippe Harousseau, Dove's marketing director on the "Campaign for Real Beauty," told the press, "It is our belief that beauty comes in different shapes, sizes and ages. Our mission is to make more women feel beautiful every day by broadening the definition of beauty."[1]

---

[1]http://www.nbcnews.com/id/8757597/ns/business-us_business/t/dove-ads-real-women-getattention/#. WoDKj2aZNBw

Dove has put their bank accounts behind their mission—investing millions of dollars into ad campaigns that have flooded the biggest cities in America with images of every day women, sizes 6-14, wearing basic white bras and underwear. They've continued to push the envelope with campaigns like"Real Beauty Sketches" which some say is the most viral ad-campaign ever. The ad that promotes the concept "you're more beautiful than you think" featured an FBI-trained forensic artist who drew images based on the way the women described themselves. Then he drew the same women based on the way other people described them. The result? The women were shown that they truly are more beautiful than they think. And Dove nearly doubled their sales.

Risky business. It's something you have to be willing to do if you want to create a brand that stands out in a noisy world. Be quirky, like Aflac. Be rebellious, like Harley Davidson. Be irreverent, like Benetton. As Apple says, Think Different.

Scared? Don't be.

In case this risky business thing is giving you the willies because you're simply not the kind of CEO that's willing to build a brand around quirks, rebellion or irreverence, rest assured, you're not out of luck.

Risky business isn't always synonymous with shock value. Sometimes, it's quite the opposite. Some of the most unforgettable brands are also the most heart-centered. Take Tom's Shoes for example.

16

When founder Blake Mycoskie learned about impoverished children living without shoes, he created TOMS Shoes with the commitment of gifting a new pair of shoes to a child in need every time a pair of shoes was sold. It's called the "One for One®" campaign and its become a social movement in its own right. To date, TOMS has donated more than 60 million pairs of shoes and it's also expanded its product line and taken its giving philosophy to an entirely new level. When they launched their eyewear collection in 2011, TOMS committed to restoring sight in countries around the world through donations of prescription eyewear and medical treatments. In 2014, they launched TOMS Roasting Co. which has since provided over 335,000 weeks of safe water in 6 countries thanks to the purchases made by coffee enthusiasts. Most recently, TOMS Bag Collection sales have afforded them the opportunity to support safe birth services for over 25,000 mothers.

Sure, Blake could have created just another shoe company that sells cool shoes and lines investors' pocketbooks. But that's not the kind of risky business Blake has chosen to create. And if you want to create an unforgettable brand, it's likely not the type of business you'll create either.

KEY TAKEAWAYS

- The world's most unforgettable brands take risks.
- Risky business isn't always synonymous with shock value.
- Some of the most unforgettable brands are also the most heart-centered.

Chapter Three

FIVE SUCCESS KEYS

19

/3/

FIVE SUCCESS KEYS

When it comes to marketplace seduction, some brands own it. To their competitors, they're untouchable. To their prospects and customers, they're magnetic. They beckon prospects with their words and images. And they make offers prospects simply cannot refuse.

If you want to create an unforgettable brand, you need to know about a company called Brand Finance. Every year they publish a study that identifies the world's most powerful and valuable brands.

In 2016, the top twenty list included Apple, Google, Samsung, Amazon, Microsoft, Verizon, AT&T, Walmart, Wells Fargo, Toyota, McDonald's, BMW, Coca Cola, Facebook and more.

We all know those brands are unforgettable. What you may not know however is that one of the main reasons they're unforgettable is because they all know the five success keys.

Key #1 - Audience Mastery

Unforgettable brands know more about their audience than anyone else. They know all of the quantitative data found on the census; however, that just barely scratches the surface when it comes to what they know about their tribe. In addition to knowing they're targeting women, 25-54 years of age that live in Dallas or whatever, they bask in qualitative data—the profound psychographics that make their target audience tick.

They know:

- what their favorite television shows are
- if they run marathons or prefer surfing
- if they stay in budget-friendly motels or opt for 5 star hotels
- if they're health conscious
- what brands they can't resist
- what keeps them up at night
- what they'd wish for if a genie gave them the opportunity to make just one wish
- …and so much more.

Unforgettable brands invest substantial amounts of time and money into understanding their audience inside and out because that is what allows them to connect with their audience in a deeply personal manner.

Key #2 - Competitive Intelligence

Just like unforgettable brands know their audience at an intimate level, they also know their competitors at an intimate level.

If you're one of those business owners who says you don't have any competitors, think again. If there's anything at all that someone can buy that is capable of creating an outcome even remotely similar to the outcome your product or service creates, then you have competition. More often than not, the CEOs that claim they have no competition have a false sense of superiority in the marketplace—and that's a very dangerous thing. Yes, you may have a patent or some intellectual property that no one can touch, or you may provide a brand experience layered with special touches; however, in the end, if the *consumer* thinks there's another option that could satisfy their needs just as well as what you sell, you have competition. You don't get to determine if you have competition. Your target market does.

Assuming you have competition, it's important to understand how powerful competitive intel fuels unforgettable brands. When it comes to your competitors, you need to know:

- What their marketing messages are
- What their customer experience is like
- What credentials and certifications they have
- What media credits they have

- The details behind every service they provide
- What niche they serve
- What geographic areas they serve
- How they show up in social media
- What their pricing structure looks like
- What the marketplace says about them in their online reviews
- What the user experience is like on their website
- What they're blogging about
- What their company story is
- …and so much more.

WANT TO GET YOUR HANDS ON MY COMPETITIVE ANALYSIS TEMPLATE?

Competitive analysis is a critical component to building an unforgettable brand, but I'll be the first to tell you, it's a beastly exercise. That's why I want to make your life easier by gifting you a copy of the spreadsheet I built and use with my private clients everyday to keep tabs on their competitors. This spreadsheet takes the guesswork out of conducting your own competitive analysis and gives you insights that you can use to blow your competition out of the water again and again.

GET IT HERE >>> SizzleForce.com/CompetitiveAnalysis

Key #3 - Remarkable Brand Experiences

It doesn't matter if you visit their website, retail store, one of their destination hotels or if you get a package in the mail from them, watch their commercials or visit their Facebook page....unforgettable brands create seamless brand experiences at every touch point. And more often than not, they play into all five senses when doing so: smell, touch, taste, sound and sight.

Disney does this better than any other company in the world. It doesn't matter if you're visiting their theme park in California or in Paris, you know you're someplace magical. Mickey Mouse is the star of the show. The grounds are always in pristine condition. Fireworks light up the sky. The music makes you want to sing along. The images invite you into the world of make believe. No stone is left unturned when it comes to details.

Just yesterday when I went to Disneyland with my family, I saw Disney add to their remarkable brand experience in a new way. Now mind you, I live in Southern California and my husband is a former cast member (that's what they call their employees), so I go to Disneyland more often than some people. For the most part, I know what to expect. But during my visit yesterday, they added to their remarkable brand experience by doing something few would ever think of: they had the cast members responsible for sweeping the grounds creating art out of their collections—in the form of Mickey

Mouse! That's right—someone cared about the remarkable brand experience Disney creates enough to teach the groundskeepers how to transform a pile of dead leaves into something people want to stop and enjoy and then tell their friends about.

What can you do to create a remarkable brand experience in your company?

This is Ben, the Disney leaf artist.

Key #4 - Captivating Stories

Show me an unforgettable brand and I'll show you an unforgettable story. Every single one of them has one. And you have one, too. You may not know what it is or how to articulate it, but sit tight, we'll cover that in the next chapter. For now, know that you must identify and share your captivating story if you want to be absolutely unforgettable.

Key #5 - Always Innovating

A new angle, a new product, a new service, a new look—unforgettable brands always have something new up their sleeve. They constantly reinvent themselves, like Madonna did at the height of her career. They keep things fresh and exciting to the point that people line up in anticipation of what's next. Just look at how many people watch the new product videos every time Apple unveils it's newest thing. What new things are you dreaming up right now?

KEY TAKEAWAYS

- Unforgettable brands know more about their audience than anyone else.
- Unforgettable brands know their competitors at an intimate level.
- Unforgettable brands create seamless brand experiences at every touch point.
- Unforgettable brands share unforgettable stories.
- Unforgettable brands always have something new up their sleeve.

Chapter Four

THE ANATOMY OF AN ABSOLUTELY UNFORGETTABLE BRAND

/4/

THE ANATOMY OF AN ABSOLUTELY UNFORGETTABLE BRAND

The biggest mistake most small business owners make when building their brand is doing things out of order. Eager to "get out there and make things happen," they jump immediately into tactics before establishing a strong foundation. It reminds of the old children's story, The Three Little Pigs…you know the one:

Once upon a time there were three little pigs.

The first little pig was lazy.

He didn't want to work at all, so he built his house out of straw.

The second little pig was willing to work a little harder than the first little pig.

But not by much, as he was quite lazy, too.

He built his house out of sticks.

After the first two little pigs built their houses, they played and played and played some more.

The third little pig was a very hard worker.

While the other two pigs rushed to build houses because they wanted to play, the third little pig worked all day and built his house out of brick.

It was strong enough to withstand any threat.

One day the wolf found the homes of the three little pigs.

He could smell the pigs living inside and wanted to eat them very badly. He tried to get the first little pig to let him in to its house but the little pig wouldn't open the door.

So the wolf huffed and puffed and blew the straw house down.

The first little piggy managed to escape to the second little piggy's house before the wolf could eat him, but it was an awfully close call.

When the wolf visited the second little piggy's house he said "let me in, let me in!"

But the piggies replied, "not by the hair on our chinny, chin, chins!"

So the wolf huffed and puffed and blew the house made out of sticks down.

The two little piggies narrowly escaped the jaws of the wolf again and ran straight to the third little piggy's house.

This was the house that belonged to the piggy that built a brick house while the other piggy's took short cuts so they could play.

The wolf came upon the third piggy's house and demanded that they let him in,

To which they replied, "not by the hair of our chinny, chin, chins!"

So the wolf huffed and puffed and tried to blow the house down.

But it didn't work.

So he huffed and puffed again.

And again and again and again until he couldn't huff and puff anymore.

He could not blow the house down.

He tried to get in the house through the chimney instead, but the three little pigs outsmarted him and ended up eating the wolf for dinner instead.

Which little piggy are you? Are you so eager to get out and play that you're not building the house you need to survive the attacks of the wolves (otherwise known as your competitors) that will come to eat you at some point in your entrepreneurial journey?

We know what happens to piggies that play too soon. Don't be that kind of piggy. Instead, be like the most successful entrepreneurs and build your house out of brick. It will serve you far better.

Laying Your Bricks

Not too long ago I did a little informal research study and asked a small group of entrepreneurs what their biggest marketing frustrations were. The overwhelming majority shared the same concern: "There's just so much to know and so much do. Facebook, LinkedIn, Twitter, Pinterest, YouTube, Instagram, e-mails, funnels, opt-ins, landing pages, podcasts, blogs, speaking engagements, networking events, and, and, and…. We don't know what to do first," they cried.

I get it. There really *is* so much to do. The good news? Rome wasn't built in a day and your success story doesn't have to be either. The most unforgettable brands build their house one brick at a time, and you should, too.

The key is to know which brick to lay first. And which brick to lay second, third, and fourth until you've built a house that's so stable, ain't nothin' gonna blow it down. That's what we're going to cover now.

Your Brick-Laying Strategy

Once you've identified the product or service you're going to sell, the first brick you need to lay is that of your ideal client. You need to know *exactly* who you're going to sell your product or service to. I touched on this briefly in chapter 3 when I wrote about audience mastery but in the following chapters we're going to get down and dirty with this topic. Because once you know your ideal clients, I mean *really, really know* them, you open the door to unlimited opportunities.

Next you need to identify your differentiators. If you haven't downloaded my free competitive analysis template yet, you really need to do that. It will make identifying your differentiators so much easier. Before you can know how you're different, you need to have a crystal clear picture of what your competitors are doing. Grab my free competitive analysis tool now to get started. You'll find it at SizzleForce.com/CompetitiveAnalysis

Once you've got your ideal client and differentiators nailed, you'll want to create your brand voice. Your brand voice will help you deeply connect with your ideal clients in a way that feels very natural to you and completely irresistible to them.

With your brand voice clearly defined, the next step is to name your company. Your brand name is the very first thing people see when looking at your company. And as the old saying goes, "you never get a second chance to make a first impression." That's why choosing an absolutely unforgettable name must be a non-negotiable item on your to do list.

Armed with your perfect company name, now you'll want to create your brand promise. In many cases, your brand promise can also become a tagline that will instantly set you apart in a noisy world. Can you tell me who said "when it absolutely, positively has to be there overnight?" And who said "Your pizza in 30 minutes or it's free?" Yep, you guessed it—FedEx and Dominoes coined those phrases DECADES ago...but you still remember them, don't you? That's the power of a brand promise.

Next you'll want to create your Unique Branded Secret™, otherwise known as your UBS. This is your step-by-step process for doing what you do every day. Here's the thing, no one does what you do the same exact way you do it. And it's that special twist you put on your process that makes you so special! We need to identify that process and give it a fancy name so you have another powerful differentiator in your tool belt.

Once you have your UBS, it's time to dig into my very favorite part of brand-building—crafting your story. This is the content that you'll place on the "about us" page of your website. You'll also likely integrate it into your speeches, your social media profiles, your book and so many other things. Your story is the core of the heart-centered connections you make with your target market.

After you craft your story, it's important to break it down into bite-sized pieces. You need to craft an absolutely unforgettable bio and networking commercial that will drive your ideal clients straight to your doorstep. That's what we'll do next.

Once you've completed all of these steps, you've built your brick house. Now you're ready to jump into the tactical side of marketing—when you implement everything and show the world that *you really are the bomb*. The clarity and confidence you have at this point will be so obvious to outsiders, the wolves won't even try to blow your brick house down. Because they know they won't be able to.

Boom. That's how it's done, ladies and gentlemen.

Now, let's do a deep dive into each of these bricks so we can get you on your way.

KEY TAKEAWAYS

- The biggest mistake most small business owners make when building their brand is doing things out of order.
- Your brick-laying strategy will require you to know your ideal clients, identify your differentiators, create your brand voice, name your company, create your brand promise, create your Unique Branded Secret™, craft your story, and craft an unforgettable bio and networking commercial.

Chapter Five

THE RICHES ARE IN THE NICHES

/5/

THE RICHES ARE IN THE NICHES

Unfortunately, the idea of niching is troublesome to many small business owners. First, most biz owners don't know what to niche in, because they don't know who their ideal client is. And since they don't know who they're targeting, they don't know how to meet their needs. This results in them wasting obscene amounts of time and money trying to sell to people who aren't going to buy. It's maddening! And I'm a firm believer that it's time to stop the madness! Let's identify your ideal client so you can claim your niche and finally stop wasting your time and money chasing all the wrong people!

Before you can know who your ideal client *is*, you need to understand who your ideal client *is not*. A number of years ago I went to a networking meeting that I'll never forget. It was time to share our 60 second commercials. The lady to my right stood up and said she sold skincare and that she could help "anyone with skin." Yes, her statement got her a few chuckles, but did she get any business? Or any referrals? Or any anything other than the chuckles? Nope. Nada. Nothing.

At that same meeting, a physical therapist stood up and said she was looking for introductions to people struggling with knee pain. I immediately thought of my husband's aunt, who has struggled with severe knee pain for years now. Had she lived locally, I most certainly would have made an introduction, but the distance made that prohibitive in this particular situation. Regardless, do you see what happened as a result of the physical therapist's willingness to niche down? Within seconds, she had almost everyone in the room thinking of someone they could introduce her to. Now bear in mind, the PT didn't say she *wouldn't* help someone with shoulder pain or back pain or some other issue. She can still work in all of those areas. But because she was laser-focused in her 'ask,' she got laser-focused leads.

When you know who your ideal client is, you can articulate that at your networking groups, in your ads, all over your website, in your social media activity, etc. And the people that have a need and see that you can provide a solution will be instantly attracted to you! Niching doesn't limit you. It opens up the floodgates to more business than you know what to do with!

So who is your ideal customer—your niche? Simply stated, your ideal customer knows they want or need your product or service (you don't have to convince them) and they value what you're selling enough to pay for it (they're not freebie hunters!) Furthermore, they make doing what you do so financially and emotionally rewarding that you can't WAIT to begin your workday (no negative nellies allowed)!

When I work with my private clients, I often start our working relationship off by completing an ideal client discovery session with them. We begin by identifying the clients that have spent the most money with them. We document their names and how much they've spent to date and look for commonalities. For example, if we find that their most profitable clients have all spent $5000 or more, we make a note of that.

We've only answered a couple of very top level questions at this point but we've already gathered some information that's so important. We know the most profitable clients are all spending $5000+. That tells us anyone that is looking to invest hundreds as opposed to thousands is the wrong client. We've weeded out bargain hunters (people that might compare their services to the low price leader) as well as the people who don't value their expertise enough to invest several thousand dollars in it.

In step two we identify the customers they've enjoyed working with the most and why. Was it something about their personality? If so, what? Was it the way they handled their payments? Was it the fact that they referred their friends? What made the experience of working with them so enjoyable? It's important to be as specific as possible when answering these questions because we really want to get a laser-focused picture of the ideal client now.

Now we look for patterns again. Our answers reveal that our clients all spend at least $5,000 for services and we also see that they loved working with them because they paid on time, were all highly communicative and they all happened to be professional service providers. In addition they were all between 35-50 years old and 4/5 were women.

Our ideal client picture is beginning to take shape. We're only two steps into this and look how far we've already come!

Now that we know who their most profitable and most enjoyable clients have been to date, we'll write a fictitious classified ad in an effort to find more ideal clients. The headline of the ad will read, "WANTED: IDEAL CLIENTS."

As we write the ad, we'll consider the patterns we recognized as we identified their most profitable clients as well as those they enjoyed working with the most. We'll also consider how they might describe the person that would benefit from their product/service the most. At this point, we'll think in terms of demographics (gender, education, ethnicity, age, employment status, location and other quantitative characteristics) and psychographics (lifestyle, attitudes, aspirations, values, opinions, beliefs, motivations, and other psychological criteria that cannot be quantified.) Let me show you an example:

"WANTED: IDEAL CLIENTS"

- age 35-50
- female
- willing to invest $5,000+ in services
- financially stable

- highly communicative
- professional service provider
- resident of San Diego county
- business owner
- lacks the time to conduct the research she needs to complete her job
- believes she should not be dabbling in areas outside of her core gifting

Next, we'll identify the social media sites their ideal clients use frequently, the magazines/newspapers they read (online or offline) and the programs they watch on television. Since it's unlikely they'll know this info off the top of their head, I'll usually call some of their top clients for them and say something along the lines of, "Client A loves working with you so much and she wants to help more people like you. Would you be willing to answer a few questions for me so we can learn more about the things people like you enjoy?" I've never had anyone turn me down when I asked this question. In fact, most are delighted to help. When you ask your top clients, those you've developed a stellar relationship with because you've provided outstanding service, to help you, they almost always will.

As a result of this exercise we learn things like they all have Facebook accounts that they check several times per week for social reasons. Professionally they rely on LinkedIn. None of them read newspapers. About half said they subscribe to magazines—those included Real Simple and Oprah. 4/5 said they listen to talk radio.

Next, we'll jump on Google and search for what's called "media kits." These are target market research goldmines. The media companies that compile them invest millions of dollars in customer research every year. Fortunately for us, they share their findings publicly—allowing us to hi-jack (don't worry, it's perfect legal) it and use it for our own purposes. These media kits will often reveal basic demographics as well as thorough psychographic data that will mirror your ideal clients. And it won't cost you a dime to get it.

For example, one media kit says its audience is:

- 77% Women
- 59% Ages 25-54
- 34% Moms
- $71K Median household income
- 85% College educated
- 71% Homeowners

Next, we'll compare and contrast these findings with another media kit that belongs to a media outlet our top clients share an affinity for. Here's an example of what we might find out about their audience:

- 53% age 25-54
- 36% children at home
- $67,944 Median HHI
- 72% College Educated

Since we can see the median household income and college education stats are pretty similar between the two media outlets, we're going to add this demographic info to our ideal client description. Now it's going to look like this:

- be age 25-54 (I'm broadening it a bit due to my research)
- be female
- be willing to invest $5,000+ in services
- be financially stable
- be highly communicative
- be a professional service provider
- be a resident of San Diego county
- be a business owner
- lack the time to conduct the research she needs completed to do her job
- believe she should not be dabbling in areas outside of her core gifting
- have a median HHI of $70,000
- be college educated

Next, we'll consider what problems their ideal clients share that they can help them solve. We're going to do this by looking at the history of their previous clients. We've already identified one problem and that is the fact that our ideal client lacks the time she needs to conduct the research needed to complete her job. We know we can solve that problem for her. As we continue exploring common problems, we'll learn things such as:

- they don't feel equipped to do their own research
- they aren't professional researchers
- even if they had all the time in the world, they fear they would overlook critical information because they don't know what they don't know.
- They need help completing research but not enough to justify hiring a full-time employee.

We now have a pretty clear idea of who their ideal client is:

- age 35-50
- female
- willing to invest $5,000+ in services
- financially stable
- highly communicative
- a professional service provider
- a resident of San Diego county
- a business owner
- lacks the time to conduct the research she needs completed to do her job
- believes she should not be dabbling in areas outside of her core gifting
- has a median HHI of $70,000
- college educated
- concerned that she doesn't have the skills to do the proper research
- needs temporary full-time help in 3 month increments

Now we're going to bring their ideal client to life by giving her a name (I'll choose Sarah) and finding a stock photo that looks like her. I'm going to run each and every marketing decision I make past "Sarah" moving forward.

And that's how you identify your ideal client.

WANT TO GET YOUR HANDS ON MY ULTIMATE NICHE FINDER TOOL?

Ready to discover the niche you were born to serve? Look no further than this tool that will position you to profit more and spend less.

GET IT FOR FREE NOW >>> SizzleForce.com/NicheFinder

KEY TAKEAWAYS

- Niching allows you to stop wasting your time and money chasing all the wrong people.
- Before you can know who you ideal client is, you need to understand who your ideal client is not.
- Your ideal client knows they want or need your product/service.
- Your ideal clients value what you're selling enough to pay for it.
- Your ideal clients make doing what you do so financially and emotionally rewarding that you can't WAIT to begin your workday.
- You can get my Ultimate Niche Finder template for free at SizzleForce.com/NicheFinder

Chapter Six

YOUR DIFFERENTIATING FACTOR

/6/

YOUR DIFFERENTIATING FACTOR

You've got competition. A lot of it. Small business owners that haven't taken the time to discover their differentiators (and learn how to articulate them) often find themselves competing on price alone. And that's a slippery slope in a fierce marketplace where brand loyalty is largely a past time and there is always, *always* someone that's willing to work for less than you. That's why it's so important to discover your differentiators. Right now, I'm going to help you discover your secret sauce.

Your prospects have choices. They can choose to give their money to you or they can choose to give it to your competition. Most of the time when I ask small business owners why they're different from their competition, they really don't know. They say things like "I'm passionate about what I do."

I've got to be brutally honest with you right now. Your ideal customers don't care about what you're passionate about. They care about what you can offer them. It all goes back to the old saying "what's in it for me?"

Not too long ago I was looking to hire a housekeeper. Knowing a lot of friends already have housekeepers, I decided to post something on Facebook telling my friends who I was looking for and asking if they had any recommendations. Within minutes I had a list of at least 10 housekeepers that could help me. Most of the messages I got said things like "Maria has been my housekeeper for 10 years, she's great." Those were nice and all viable options for me to consider. But then I got this referral in a private message. "Call Rita... she's Italian, and will make you meatballs... and eggplant parmesan... and she does a very good job cleaning. She's great. Her number is: XXX-XXX-XXXX."

WHAT? A housekeeper that cleans AND makes meatballs? Have I died and gone to Heaven?

The message then proceeded to tell me that she was from southern Italy...which meant her meatballs were even better than I thought they would be. I was instantly sold. Yes, I wanted my house clean but I also wanted meatballs and I didn't even know it at the time! Rita, whom I now affectionately refer to as "the meatball housekeeper" got the job. She differentiated herself. She became memorable and instantly stood out from the rest of the pack.

This is kind of a silly story but it's a powerful example of how differentiating works! So let's get into differentiating YOU!

For the third time now, I'm going to tell you to grab that competitive analysis worksheet I'm giving you for free. Why? Because it's going to equip you to stand out in a variety of ways.

And that's a really important part of making your brand absolutely unforgettable. You can grab my free competitive analysis template at SizzleForce.com/CompetitiveAnalysis.

I'm not going to get into the semantics of completing your competitive analysis now because the worksheet is really very self-explanatory, but I will give you a few tips to tap into while you're working on it.

- You can get most of the information you need from your competitor's websites and social media profiles.

- Yelp, Angie's List, Facebook reviews, LinkedIn Recommendations and Google reviews are also great places to glean additional insights. If your competitor has a physical product on Amazon for sale, be sure to check those reviews out as well.

- If you really want to pull some ninja moves and you're competing against companies that are large enough to be supporting an online advertising budget, you can get a free trial with SpyFu.com. This tool will allow you to see how much your competitors are spending on Adwords, what their SEO traffic looks like, etc.

- You may want to consider hiring someone to complete your competitive research for you. They'll call your competitors, ask any questions that you can't find answers to via your online research and document them for your review.

- The worksheet I'm giving you access to will have some categories that are irrelevant to you. I use this with all kinds of different companies and it's always evolving. That's okay. Simply delete any categories that don't apply to you.

Once you've completed the competitive analysis for your competitors, you need to do it for yourself. This can be tricky because it's hard to see yourself objectively. It may make sense to hire someone that is not associated with your company to do this for you.

After you've inserted all of the details for your competitors and yourself, scour the spreadsheet for differentiators. While you're at it, make note of any strengths, weaknesses, opportunities and threats you see.

Once you've completed the competitive analysis, you'll want to continue hunting for differentiators by creating a survey and sending it to your favorite customers. I suggest getting a free account with SurveyMonkey that will allow you to create a survey with up to 10 questions at no charge. This service allows you to collect data via weblink, email, Facebook, or even by embedding it on your site or blog.

Here are some of the questions you'll want to ask in your survey:

1. Why did you hire me instead of my competition?
2. What problem(s) did I help you solve?
3. Please describe me in 3-5 words.
4. What makes me different from other people that sell similar products/services?
5. If you were to recommend me to a friend or colleague, what would you say?

The insights you'll glean from this survey can be priceless, so do not skip this very important step!

Next, answer the following questions yourself. (I've allowed space for you to document your answers right in this book so you always know where to find them.)

1). Why did you start your business? I want you to try and pull out something emotional here. I mean, you could have done anything. You could be a mail delivery person or a firefighter or an actor but you chose to do what you do for a very specific reason. Why?

2) What did you do before you started this business? Please provide a detailed answer to this question. Rather than just stating your title and the name of the company you worked for, document what your job responsibilities were. Identify how long you worked for the company and how the company itself or the position you held is relevant to what you're doing now.

3) Do you have an office space? If so, where? Do you work virtually from your home? How many people work in your company? What are their responsibilities? Please share as many details as possible.

4) How do you stay on top of the trends and changes in your industry? Do you go to continuing education classes? Are you always first in line to purchase your ticket to the industry's annual conference?

5) Have you ever worked with any celebrities or well-known and respected clients? If so, who? Celebrity associations carry a lot of weight. Whenever you can ride on celebrity coat tails, you best do it.

6) What benefits do your customers receive as a result of working with you? Remember to really think benefits here…not features. Let's pretend you sell high-end designer jeans. A feature might be something like an unbreakable zipper or wash that won't fade. A benefit is how that feature directly impacts the customer. The unbreakable zipper means they won't have any embarrassing accidents in public. The wash that won't fade means their jeans will last and last and they won't have to buy a new pair for a very long time because these will always look brand new. You get the idea, right?

7) What are your top three professional accomplishments? Don't be shy! This is your time to shine. People aren't going to buy from you because you're humble. They're going to buy from you because you're good. And they only know you're good if you tell 'em!

8) What three things do you do better than your competitors? When answering this question, please be factual and only identify things you can back up with facts. For example, saying you provide great service or that you really care about your clients won't do much for you. Those are great things; however, since you can't back them up with evidence, they really aren't helpful.

9) If you could only communicate one key message to your clients, what would it be? What is your promise to the marketplace? If you get tripped up on this part, relax. In chapter nine we'll talk all about your brand promise. You can skip this question for now and come back to it after you've read that chapter if you need to.

Now that you've answered all of these questions, and received the results of the survey you sent to your top clients, study it with an objective eye as much as you can. It's okay to ask for help if you need it! This is why my clients hire me to do this for them. It can be hard to see! Look for the things that make you unique. Sometimes something that's so important and obvious to your clients is something you can't even see. It's just so engrained in what you do that you assume everyone does it. But most don't. This is very likely your secret sauce.

One of my all-time favorite clients is a hypnotherapist. Yep, she hypnotizes people for a living. Often when she tells people she's a hypnotist they immediately wonder if she's going to make them fall into some kind of crazy trance and cluck like a chicken. But that's not what she does at all. She does incredibly powerful work that transforms lives. She has a long list of clients that she's helped—from smokers that have been addicted for decades to people that couldn't lose weight no matter what they tried and so much more.

When she really wanted to focus on growing the weight loss end of her business, we identified three differentiators for her to share with the marketplace.

1) She identifies with her clients. She has lost a ton of weight herself and kept it off using her own hypnosis strategies.

2) She's a rebel in the weight loss industry. Instead of going with the grain and marketing her services as a quick fix or trendy diet, she assumed her clients already knew that to lose weight you had to eat less and move more. So instead of focusing on that, she focuses on crushing the emotional attachments people have to food and exercise.

3) She doesn't do wheatgrass and wind chimes. (This one is my favorite!) Because of her practical approach that's based on brain-imaging technology she's able to immediately dispel the woo woo myths people believe about hypnotists and present herself as the hypnotist for "the peeps that don't do woo-woo."

What's your secret sauce?

KEY TAKEAWAYS

– Small business owners that haven't taken the time to discover their differentiators (and learn how to articulate them) often find themselves competing on price alone.

– You can grab my Competitive Analysis worksheet for free at SizzleForce.com/CompetitiveAnalysisAnalysis

– Sometimes your secret sauce is something you can't even see.

Chapter Seven

PERSONALITY MATTERS

PERSONALITY MATTERS

Want to create connections with your ideal clients in a way that feels very natural to you and completely irresistible to your ideal clients? Good! You need to create your brand voice—one of the most important components of your brand personality.

Your brand voice is an essential success strategy element because it effects how the marketplace perceives you and helps them decide if they want to do business with you or not. So let me teach you now, how to create your brand voice as well as what to do with it once you have it.

The first step is to identify your company's personality. Pretend your company is a person. If you were given the opportunity to define your company using just three adjectives, what would you say?

If you asked me about my company SizzleForce Marketing, I'd tell you it's creative, energetic and smart. It could've been adventurous, humorous and outdoorsy or possibly analytical, succinct and serious, but it's not. Just like every person has a unique personality, every company should, too. That said, how would you describe your company's personality?

Take a look at the 99 options I've listed here and circle each one that you want your brand to represent. Then, narrow it down to the top 10. And finally, pick the three most compelling personality traits that represent your brand.

1. playful	19. professional	37. simple
2. energetic	20. competitive	38. wise
3. knowledgeable	21. patient	39. optimistic
4. adventurous	22. fast	40. polished
5. humorous	23. factual	41. innovative
6. outdoorsy	24. detailed	42. liberal
7. analytical	25. accessible	43. flexible
8. succinct	26. charming	44. dramatic
9. serious	27. elegant	45. masculine
10. gentle	28. sassy	46. flexible
11. direct	29. romantic	47. purposeful
12. authoritative	30. strong	48. genuine
13. warm	31. rowdy	49. honest
14. dependable	32. ambitious	50. aggressive
15. efficient	33. courageous	51. clean
16. smart	34. compassionate	52. precise
17. imaginative	35. traditional	53. dreamy
18. compassionate	36. daring	54. light-hearted

55. reliable
56. colorful
57. tough
58. brave
59. free-thinking
60. quirky
61. casual
62. irreverent
63. silly
64. cooperative
65. logical
66. spiritual
67. rustic
68. sexy
69. modern

70. confident
71. organic
72. systematic
73. trustworthy
74. feminine
75. heartfelt
76. safe
77. enthusiastic
78. healthy
79. eloquent
80. clever
81. orderly
82. cute
83. earthy
84. modest

85. formal
86. dedicated
87. affordable
88. passionate
89. conservative
90. faithful
91. whimsical
92. relaxed
93. stylish
94. delicate
95. fiery
96. intense
97. trendy
98. disciplined
99. powerful

Once you've identified your three personality traits, you'll want to define what your traits really mean to you as a company.

I'll use my own company as an example. If my personality traits are creative, energetic and smart, I need to start by defining what creative means to SizzleForce, in just one or two sentences.

I'd say creative for us means that we think differently. We look for things most don't see. We tackle angles most people don't touch.

For energetic I'd say we're full of life and we create movement in the marketplace.

And finally, for smart I'd say we create innovative marketing solutions that make our clients feel good about their marketing and look good in the marketplace while generating an impressive return on investment.

Now it's your turn. Make a list of do's and don'ts based on your company traits and the definitions you just developed.

Trait	Do's/Don'ts

Again, using SizzleForce as an example, I've determined that we're creative which means that we think differently, look for things most don't see and take angles most people don't touch. That being the case, SizzleForce would aim to communicate in a way that inspires introspection and processing things from different vantage points. That would require a casual yet inspiring tone that's quick to make people smile. It would also require us to resist being grammar-geeks, using fancy language that you need to have a PhD to understand and coming across as corporate and stuffy.

The next step is to decide how you're going to make sure your brand voice shines in every component of your marketing—your website, your printed marketing materials, your social media presence, your videos, ads, speaking engagements, trade shows booths, etc, etc, etc.

Let me give you an example of how my company personality shows up in what I do. Last year I was given an opportunity to have a booth for SizzleForce at a big event that was filled with my target market. There were a lot of vendors there so it was especially important that my booth screamed the fact that SizzleForce is creative, energetic and smart.

A lot of other companies at that event placed a banner, a bowl of candy and some fliers at their table and had a representative of the company sitting behind the table ready to talk with people that stopped by. If I did that for Sizzle-Force, it would have been completely out of alignment with my brand because there's absolutely nothing creative, energetic or smart about that approach. Here's what I did instead:

First, I made sure my signage and fliers were creative. I used powerful language, eye-catching fonts and oversized props, like a giant margarita glass to collect business cards instead of the fishbowl that everyone else used. I did have candy at my table but it wasn't just a random assortment of whatever, I got chocolate coins wrapped in gold foil that complimented my brand visuals.

To communicate energy, I knew I needed movement at my booth. I got two clip-on desk fans and attached one to each side of the table. Then, I planted several pinwheels, in my brand colors—right in the path of the fans. Immediately, my booth came to life, because there was movement. The pinwheels caught everyone's eye as they walked by and practically created a magnetic pull to my booth.

I added an extra dose of energy to the table by creating a game. I distributed pretend money at the table throughout the event. Each bill had a number on it. Throughout the three day event, I changed the number on the chalkboard that sat on my table several times. I told everyone that got a bill that they had to continually stop by the booth throughout the event to see if their number was on the board. If it was, I gave them a very cool prize. It was magical!

Finally, I communicated that we were smart by the word choices we used when people came to the booth, the service I sold and a monitor that displayed testimonials of the results I'd generated for my other clients.

You know what happened? I created a buzz that resulted in my booth being the most profitable booth at the event. We sold more than anyone else…by a long shot. And we got enough business from the one event to break our first quarter sales record history!

I'm not telling you this to impress you. I'm telling you to impress upon you what I shared at the beginning of this chapter: Your brand voice is an essential component of your success strategy because it effects how the marketplace perceives you and helps them decide if they want to do business with you or not. When you put the time into really defining your brand and what it means and then integrating that into your marketing activities, you set yourself up for massive success.

KEY TAKEAWAYS

- Your brand voice effects how the marketplace perceives you and helps them decide if they want to do business with you or not.
- Just like every person has a unique personality, every company should, too.
- Your brand voice needs to show up in every component of your marketing.

Chapter Eight

WHAT'S IN A NAME

/8/

WHAT'S IN A NAME

When you name your company, products and/or service offerings, you need to be very intentional about it. Why? Because in many cases, your name sets the tone for how people perceive your company.

An absolutely unforgettable brand name can boast of five things:

1) **It showcases your brand promise.**

   Consider the name QuickBooks. It leaves no room for speculation. The name itself tells you the software helps you quickly manage your books—something that's very important to business owners that are spinning thousands of different plates at any given time. Another example of a great name comes from Hertz. Before everyone had GPS on their phones, they created a GPS product called NeverLost. I love how simple and clear that name is. After all, when you're traveling in the a new city, getting lost is a big concern. Hertz squashed that concern immediately with the NeverLost product.

2) **It's got personality.**

Google. Yahoo. Zappos. SizzleForce. (Pardon me for the shameless plug—I couldn't help myself.) Fun names set a tone that implies customers will have an enjoyable experience when they do business with one of these brands. And if there's anything you want when all is said and done, it's happy customers.

3) **It's short, sweet and easy to pronounce.**

Apple. Gap. Burger King. There's no guessing when it comes to how to pronounce these names and they're so simple, anyone can remember them. On the contrary, yogurt brand Fage is pronounced fa-yay, footwear brand Saucony is pronounced sock-a-nee, and we can't forget about the cray-cray person who approved the name Boehringer Ingelheim for the US market. Just *try* to say that out loud. I dare you. The correct pronunciation is bear-ring-her ing-ell-hime. But who would have ever known? If you don't want people butchering your brand name every time they say it, make it short, sweet and easy to pronounce.

4) **It's evergreen.**

Nothing kills a name faster than centering it around a trend that you didn't create. Does anything scream mid 90's or early 2000's more than X Games, eHarmony, or iAnything? If you're building a company around a trend that you didn't create with no intention whatsoever of carrying it into the next decade, than go ahead and name it around a trend. If you're naming something that you want to last, avoid trends like the plague. Note: Apple created the iPhone, iPad, etc. trend—it's theirs and everyone knows it. That's the only reason they can use it so successfully now.

5) **It's indestructible when translated into different languages.**

There's an Iranian company that manufactures a washing machine detergent called "snow" in Farsi. The problem is that when you translate it into English, it means barf. That's right—barf. Need I say more? (Many thanks to AdWeek for bringing this fabulous bit of information to my attention way back in 2009. I'm still laughing.)

Why You Might Need To Change Your Name

In an ideal world, you'll never have to change your name. But the truth is, a lot of companies have no other choice. Here are 5 of the most common reasons why companies change their name (and maybe you should change yours).

1. **They have a bad reputation.**

I know of a business owner in San Diego that owns a restaurant overlooking the ocean. It's a prime location in a tourist hot spot and because of that, it gets a lot of foot traffic. The problem? The owner. The owner is toxic and he creates one horrific customer experience after another. But instead of changing his way of doing business, he simply changes the restaurant. He gives it a new menu, new name, new interior design, new, new, new. And then, once he gets enough lethal reviews, he closes it down and starts the process all over again. #TrueStory

2. **They're merging with another company.**

    Often times a merger requires a brand update to reflect changes in leadership, additional service offerings, new initiatives, etc.

3. **They've outgrown their niche or are entering a new market.**

    Let's say there's a company called San Diego Pencil Sharpeners. Now, that's a horrible company name but bear with me. If they call themselves that, and then expand to Orlando or New York City, their name just isn't going to work very well for them anymore. When your company outgrows the name you started it with, sometimes you have to let it go.

4. **Political or cultural shifts.**

    This is an interesting one. At one point there was a mobile payments company, backed by some of the big cell phone carriers, originally named Isis. At the time, it wasn't a big deal but can you imagine if that was still their name today? Would you want to send your money to Isis?? This company was forced to rebrand because of something completely out of their control. It happens more often than you'd think.

5. **They need to level up or modernize.**

    Some of the biggest companies in the world originally had absolutely atrocious names. A bad name gets you nowhere fast. But a good name, with a solid marketing plan behind it, can make you a household brand. Keep reading to learn what Pepsi, Google, Nike, Hertz, and Sony all once had in common.

There are probably many other reasons to consider changing your name but really, only *you* can decide if/when it's time to do so.

How important is it to keep the "well known in a small niche name?"

No one can determine how important your company name is to your existing customers but you. That said, here are a couple of things to consider:

- **Sometimes, changing the name is the best thing a company can do.**

  In fact, some of the biggest household names out there have done it!

  - ¤ Pepsi used to be called Brad's Drink. The founder, Caleb Bradham, decided to name his drink after himself (because who wouldn't?) and then somewhere along the way, someone with way more creativity came up with the name Pepsi, they rebranded, and the rest is history.
  - ¤ Google used to be called Back Rub. Yes, really. Look it up. It's true.
  - ¤ Nike was once Blue Ribbon Sports.
  - ¤ Hertz Rent-A-Car used to be Drive-Ur-Self.
  - ¤ Sony used to be Tokyo Tsushin Kogyo.
  - ¤ SizzleForce Marketing (yay!) used to be Impressions Marketing Studio (yuck!)

I broke all of my own rules when I named my company origi-nally. I did what I thought I *should* do rather than being au-thentic and heart-centered. I named my business, did all the paperwork, got all of my marketing materials done and then immediately started kicking myself because I hated the name. I hated introducing my business because the name had no zing and it didn't represent what I wanted my busi-ness to represent. And then there came that horrible day when I went to a networking meeting and met another mar-keter with an almost *identical* company name and a little part of me died right then and there. As a marketer, this is a car-dinal sin!

If you're just getting started and you haven't yet named your company, please...don't make the mistake I made! It is time-consuming and expensive to recreate a brand! Save yourself the hassle and do as I suggest the first time! If you've already named your company and found that it's just not working for you, it may be time to rename. Whether or not you *should*, is a question only you can answer.

If you do decide to rename your business, there are a few things you need to know:

- **It can be expensive.** You'll probably need to have your logo redesigned, new business cards created, and have your website, social media art, print marketing materials and more changed. It's an investment.
- Communication is key. Be sure to clearly communicate the change, and the reasons for the change, to your ex-

isting customers, as well as any other businesses you partner with. You'll want to do this mostly through social media and a great email nurturing campaign that keeps them in the loop so they know you haven't disappeared.

There's a whole lot more that goes into creating a brand name that's absolutely unforgettable, but this should be enough to get you going in the right direction. Your brand name is going to follow you wherever you go. Be intentional when choosing it.

KEY TAKEAWAYS

- When you name your company, products and/or service offerings, you need to be very intentional about it.
- An absolutely unforgettable brand name showcases your brand promise, has personality, and is short, sweet, easy to pronounce, evergreen and indestructible when translated into different languages.
- You may need to change your company name if you have a bad reputation, are merging, have outgrown your niche, are entering a new market, operating in the midst of political/cultural shifts that relate to your name or if it's time to level up or modernize.

Chapter Nine

PINKY PROMISE

PINKY PROMISE

Forgive me in advance, but it's time for me to share the cold, hard truth with you. People don't want to buy your product or service. They just don't.

Ouch! Did I really just write that? Well yes, I did. But don't get your panties in a bunch over it because I'm not saying what you think I am.

People *do* want to buy something you offer, you just need to understand what it is. If it's not your product and it's not your service, what is it? Hint: it's not something they can see. Nor is it something they can touch, smell, hear or taste.

People want to buy what you sell because doing so gives them *hope*. Hope that your product or service will solve whatever problem or satisfy whatever desire they have. That's where your brand promise comes in. When you learn how to articulate the solution you offer—the hope you sell—in just a few, powerful words, you have what we marketers refer to as your brand promise.

To create your brand promise, we need to revisit some of the topics discussed in previous chapters and also do a little new work. Let's dig in:

1) Turn back to chapter five, "The Riches Are In The Niches." Remember when you identified the common problems your ideal clients share? Write those down again here. If I were a marriage and family therapist I might have said, "many of my ideal clients are in a strained marriage and many of them fight often about money."

2) Identify how these problems make your ideal clients *feel*. You want to get really raw, honest and specific here. The more real you are, the better your outcome will be. A marriage and family therapist might say something along the lines of, "They feel sad because they miss the relationship they used to have with their spouse. They also miss the romantic dates, thoughtful gestures and companionship they once had. They might also be scared. If there's not enough money, they might be afraid that they're going to lose their house or not have money

to pay for groceries. Finally, they're also probably very angry and likely resenting their spouse because of the way he/she handles money."

3) Write down your detailed ideal client description.

4) Document your SMART goals. You need to identify at least 2 goals. When doing so, make sure you write them in a way that's **S**pecific, **M**easurable, **A**ttainable, **R**ealistic, and **T**ime-sensitive. As a marriage and family therapist I might say, "My SMART goal is to generate 100 new leads for a class I'm teaching called, "Money and Marriage—How to Develop Healthy Financial Habits And Live To Tell About It."

5) Write down your 3 most powerful differentiators based on the work you did in chapter 6. As a therapist I could say, "I am teaching a class that I created the curriculum for called, 'Money and Marriage—How to Develop Healthy Financial Habits And Live To Tell About It'. A second differentiator could be the fact that before I became a therapist, I was actually a financial planner for 10 years. Boom. That's powerful given my target market.

6) Continue revisiting the work you did in Chapter 6 and document how your differentiators benefit your clients. As a marriage and family therapist I might say, "the fact that I was a financial planner before I became a therapist shows that I have a solid background in finance. This is a benefit to my ideal clients because their #1 problem is that they're fighting all the time about money! I can marry my financial training with my training as a therapist and help them establish healthy money communication strategies and habits that will result in both the husband and wife feeling like the vast majority of their needs and wants are being met—and as a result, they'll have a more peaceful home, they'll restore the companionship as-

pect of their relationship, and the fear and resentment that once caused major issues will be squashed."

7) Identify how your ideal clients *feel* when they experience the benefits of your products/services. Add numbers to this whenever possible. A therapist would want to consider how her ideal clients feel when they realize the benefits of restored companionship, peace and joy. She'd want to consider the practical ways that will play out in day-to-day living that her target audience can relate to.

8) Cruise back to the work you did on your brand voice. What three traits represent your brand most? If the therapist were completing this she might say her 3 top traits are humor, intelligence and honesty.

9) Document how your brand traits show up in your company. Our therapist might say humor shows up in her company by the way she titles her classes and products. Intelligence might show up based on the solutions she provides. And honesty might show up based on the culture of her classroom and community as a whole.

10) Determine what your unwavering commitment to your clients is. If you do nothing else, what do you absolutely, positively guarantee you WILL do for them? Continuing on with my example for the therapist, I'll say her promise is to give her clients smart, honest financial marriage counseling in a humorous manner.

Once you've completed the ten steps identified above, it will be time to start crafting your brand promise. But first, let me give you a little inspiration in the form of existing brand promises other companies have made a fortune from.

GEICO's brand promise is: 15 Minutes Could Save You 15 Percent or More on Car Insurance.

Marriott's brand promise is: Quiet Luxury. Crafted Experiences. Intuitive Service.

BMW's brand promise is that their car is the Ultimate Driving Machine.

Walmart's promise is: Save Money. Live Better.

Saddleback Leather Company's promise is: They'll fight over it when you're dead.

Do you see how the personality of each of these brands comes through when you read their brand promise? Now, it's your turn to develop yours. Give yourself full creative freedom when you're coming up with ideas here. Don't censor yourself during the brainstorming session—some of the best brand promises are born from the most bizarre brainstorms!

How To Know When You've Crafted An Absolutely Unforgettable Brand Promise

You know you've created a winning brand promise when:

- The benefit is clear
- It reflects your brand voice

- It's memorable
- It's specific
- It differentiates you
- It's 7 words or less

KEY TAKEAWAYS

- People don't want to buy your product or service.
- People want to buy what you sell because doing so gives them hope.
- Some of the best brand promises are born from the most bizarre brainstorms!
- You know you've crafted an absolutely unforgettable brand promise when the benefit is clear, it reflects your brand voice, it's memorable, it's specific, it differentiates you and it's 7 words or less.

Chapter Ten

YOUR SECRET SYSTEM

/10/

YOUR SECRET SYSTEM

You may or may not know this by now, but you have a secret system for the way you do things. Maybe you've documented it. Maybe you haven't. Maybe you're not even sure if you have one, but I guarantee, you do. And when you brand your secret system, you have another extremely powerful differentiator in your marketing toolbox. I call it your Unique Branded Secret™.

The first step to identifying your secret system is to slow down and carefully analyze every step of the process you take when delivering the solutions your ideal clients are buying from you. This is kind of tedious but it's really, really important, so bear with me.

One of my clients is a very high-level executive coach that often works with the CEO's of Fortune 100 companies. She operates in an incredibly competitive market, so having a Unique Branded Secret™ was critical to setting her apart in the marketplace.

The Unique Branded Secret™ I created for her is called the D.Y.N.A.M.I.C. Executive™ Coaching program and she calls it her 7-step approach to coaching at the senior leadership level. It's the success formula she's used while coaching executive leaders at companies including AT&t, Raytheon, Mattel, Wells Fargo and more and continues to use to this day.

The word "dynamic" in the D.Y.N.A.M.I.C. Executive program™ is an acronym for the process she takes every client through when she works with them.

She begins with the "discovery" phase, which is the letter "d" in "dynamic." This is when she creates a framework for how she'll serve the client at the highest level.

Next she moves into the "yields" phase, which is the letter "y" in "dynamic." This is when she determines the ROI the client is expecting, benchmarks, goals, etc.

Then she moves into the "navigation" phase, the letter "n" in "dynamic."

At this point she charts a course to move the client from where they are to where they want to be as a result of the work she does with them.

Next, she moves them into the "application" phase...the letter "a" in "dynamic". At this point she's facilitating transformative coaching sessions where her clients move from learning to applying what they've learned in real world situations.

After that. she jumps into the "maximizing" phase, the letter "m" in "dynamic." This is when everyone involved in her service gains insight into how it's translating into behavioral shifts and team development.

Next, she starts to "ingrain" the shifts for long-term sustainability in the workplace. This is the letter "I" in "dynamic."

Finally she wraps it all up with "consciousness", where she ensures her clients (and their team members) are conscious and aware of what it takes to sustain high level performance and thinking.

If you look really carefully at her process, while she does it in a way that no one else can totally duplicate because they're not her, the truth is, her process is probably similar to other processes many executive coaches follow. They just haven't taken the time to analyze and brand their processes. I say that to impress upon you the fact that *your* process doesn't necessarily have to be some ground-breaking new approach. It's simply YOUR approach. And if no one else in your industry is articulating this approach the way you are, you've equipped yourself with a significant advantage.

How To Create Your Unique Branded Secret™

The approach I took with the client I just referred to was just one of many ways to craft your Unique Branded Secret™. I do encourage you to give it a try. Look back at the words you circled in Chapter Three: Personality Matters. Chances are, you can take one of those words and develop your system around it. One of my favorite things to do in Google is to search for things like "verbs that begin with the letter M" (or whatever letter you're working with.) I almost always find a verb that reflects a part of my client's process when I do this. Give it a whirl.

If the word-to-acronym approach isn't working for you, you might want to try something that many people find a little easier. For example, you can always do "the ABC's of ..." or "the 1, 2, 3 of ..." or "the 5 (insert letter of your choice) of success" or "the four seasons of (insert what you do). For example, if you're a dating coach you could create a system called "the four seasons of love," where you break down your process as a dating coach of getting people from the first date to the long term commitment, in four distinct steps. Or, if you're a professional that helps kids get into college, you could create a system called "the 3 A's to Acceptance" where you break down your process of getting kids into the college of their choice into three steps that all start with the letter "A." That one is kind of fun because you get a little wordplay in there too because everyone knows to get in the best schools you have to get all A's.

When it comes to creating your Unique Branded Secret™ there are no hard and fast rules aside from one—make it memorable! So have fun with this!

KEY TAKEAWAYS

- You have a secret system for the way you do things.
- If no one else in your industry is articulating your approach the way you are, you equip yourself with a significant advantage.
- When it comes to creating your Unique Branded Secret™ there are no hard and fast rules aside from one—make it memorable!

THE HEARTBEAT OF YOUR ABSOLUTELY UNFORGETTABLE BRAND

/11/

THE HEARTBEAT OF YOUR ABSOLUTELY UNFORGETTABLE BRAND

The heartbeat of every unforgettable brand is a story.

People love stories. We like to tell them. We like to hear them. People watch movies and T.V. shows and watch live theater and read books because *everyone loves a good story!* Stories captivate us because they make us *feel* things.

But stories aren't just for entertainment. Businesses tell stories all the time. A good story gives your small business a big voice. It connects the dots between your ideal clients and you. A captivating brand story humanizes your company because it taps into emotions. And given that 90% of purchases are made based on emotions rather than logic, it's really important for you to learn how to articulate an emotionally-charged story for your company.

Every brand has a story, yet many don't tell it because they think it's not interesting enough. But there's something very magnetic about authenticity and transparency in today's business world. If you dare to take off your mask and invite people into your true story, you'll create authentic connections that can carry your company for years to come.

The Start-Up Story

There are two types of stories that win customer's hearts again and again. The first one is what I call "the start-up story." If anyone knows how to tell an awesome start-up story, it's Warby Parker. Here's how their start-up story reads on their website:

Warby Parker was founded with a rebellious spirit and a lofty objective: to offer designer eyewear at a revolutionary price, while leading the way for socially conscious businesses.

Every idea starts with a problem. Ours was simple: glasses are too expensive. We were students when one of us lost his glasses on a backpacking trip. The cost of replacing them was so high that he spent the first semester of grad school without them, squinting and complaining. (We don't recommend this.) The rest of us had similar experiences, and we were amazed at how hard it was to find a pair of great frames that didn't leave our wallets bare. Where were the options?

It turns out there was a simple explanation. The eyewear industry is dominated by a single company that has been able to keep prices artificially high while reaping huge profits from consumers who have no other options.

We started Warby Parker to create an alternative.

By circumventing traditional channels, designing glasses in-house, and engaging with customers directly, we're able to provide higher-quality, better-looking prescription eyewear at a fraction of the going price.

We believe that buying glasses should be easy and fun. It should leave you happy and good-looking, with money in your pocket.

We also believe that everyone has the right to see.

Almost one billion people worldwide lack access to glasses, which means that 15% of the world's population cannot effectively learn or work. To help address this problem, Warby Parker partners with non-profits like VisionSpring to ensure that for every pair of glasses sold, a pair is distributed to someone in need.

There's nothing complicated about it. Good eyewear, good outcome.

Here's what makes the Warby Parker start up story so compelling:

- It levels the playing field right off the bat, illustrating how one of their one of their founders is just like a guy most of us know in real life—a broke college student that lost his glasses and suffered for a period of time because he couldn't afford to replace them.
- It showcases collective agreement that there's a problem out there that needs to be solved.

- It identifies the root of the problem and introduces the enemy—the big, bad company that dominates the eyewear industry and forces people to pay way too much for their eyewear.
- It introduces the hero and his mission.
- It explains how the hero is able to accomplish his mission.
- It tells the reader how the hero's product will positively impact your life.
- It tugs at your heart strings and showcases social responsibility.
- It summarizes the mission in simple terms that everyone can understand and appreciate.

How To Write Your Start Up Story

There's no reason to reinvent the wheel. We've identified a powerful start up story and dissected it line by line. Writing your own should be fairly easy once you answer these questions:

1. What happened that made you realize there was a problem in the marketplace that needed to be solved?

2. Who did you connect with that agreed this was indeed a problem that needed a solution? How did they experience the problem?

3. What was the root of the problem? Who was the enemy and what were they doing?

4. Who are you and why were you compelled to solve this problem?

5. What steps did you take to actually solve the problem?

6. What do you believe about the product/service you sell?

7. How are you showcasing social responsibility?

8. In just a few words, how can you summarize what you sell and how it makes the world a better place?

The Why You Get Out Of Bed Story

The second type of story that wins customer's hearts again and again is what I call the "why you get out of bed story." The Volunteers of America website does a stellar job of explaining exactly why they get out of bed every day on their website page "why we do what we do." Their story reads like this:

We are Volunteers of America.

And we are the first to step forward,

taking on the most crushing problems.

The dire.

The hopeless.

The untouchable.

And we make a difference.

Because we not only perceive the burdens of others,

we know firsthand what it means to make them lighter.

This is why we do what we do.

Our story is long and rich.

And widely unknown.

But we're not chasing fame. Or glory.

Our lives are meant for service.

For lifting up the broken-hearted.

For finding the lost.

For reaching out with mercy and compassion

to those who thought they were beyond reach.

For uplifting all our lives.

This is why we do what we do.

Every day, we see our brothers and sisters

lying beaten and bruised on their own roads to Jericho.

We act because we're trained.

We're impassioned.

We're honored.

This is why we do what we do.

Like our Great Exemplar,

we go among the unclean,

the broken,

the forgotten

and the outcast

and we use our lives

to make theirs better.

This is why we do what we do.

Here's what makes the Volunteers of America's why you get out of bed story so compelling:

1. It uses words that stir the emotions (hopeless, untouchable, lost, impassioned, honored, broken, forgotten and outcast, amongst others.)
2. In the first few lines it says who they are, what they do and who they do it for.
3. It explains what they're not motivated by.
4. It showcases their core beliefs.

How To Write Your Why You Get Out Of Bed Story

Again, after you answer just a few questions, you'll have the nuts and bolts you need to create your own magnetic story.

1. What words describe the people you help? Make a list of at least 10, preferably more.

2. What is the name of your company?

3. What do you do specifically?

4. Who do you serve?

5. Why are you doing something about this problem? Why not let someone else take care of it?

6.   What are you *not* motivated by?

7.   What are your core beliefs?

Once you have your start up story and your why you get out of bed story, you have the core stories you need to create the heartbeat of your absolutely unforgettable brand.

KEY TAKEAWAYS

- A good story gives your small business a big voice and connects the dots between your ideal clients and you.
- 90% of purchases are made based on emotions rather than logic.
- If you dare to take off your mask and invite people into your true story, you'll create authentic connections that can carry your company for years to come.
- Once you have your start up story and your why you get out of bed story, you have the core stories you need to create the heartbeat of your absolutely unforgettable brand.

Chapter Twelve

WHAT TO DO NOW

/12/

WHAT TO DO NOW

Now that you've completed the most essential steps of creating your absolutely unforgettable brand, it's time to pull it all together.

I know how it goes—just as you're feeling all fired up about what you've created, and filled with visions of what this means for your company moving forward, life hits you in the face. You lose a huge account. A critical member of your team quits. You get sued. Unfortunately, these things happen, but one of the best ways to stay on track regardless of whatever life throws your way, is to encapsulate the most important aspects of your brand into one handy little document. It can be used to quickly get new team members up to speed. It's also a fabulous overview to give to any freelancers you hire—especially those assisting you with your website, copywriting, public relations, social media, video marketing, advertising or anything else that falls under the marketing umbrella.

That's why I've created the Brand Blueprint for you. The information in this easy-to-use, fill-in-the-blank worksheet should be given to your graphic designer for inclusion in your brand guidelines (also commonly referred to as your style guide).

In many cases, brand guidelines only reflect the visual identify of a company—think logo, colors, font styles, images, etc. While all of that is very important, the work you've completed as a result of reading this book is equally important. I invite you to download this blueprint now, fill it out and then ask your designer to add it to your style guide. It will help you stay focused and centered on what really matters—getting noticed and attracting more of your ideal clients—for years to come.

DOWNLOAD YOUR FREE BRAND BLUEPRINT

Gain clarity, ooze confidence and create a bridge between your ideal clients and your company with this FREE, fill-in-the-blank brand blueprint.

GET IT FOR FREE NOW >>> SizzleForce.com/Brand Blueprint

In Closing

Thank you for reading this book. I hope you understand how absolutely unforgettable you are and how much the world needs what you have to offer. Now, it's time to take what you've learned and put it to good use.

Remember, no one ever changed the world by hiding. You

were created to do amazing things. You have to get out there and share your greatness in order to make a difference. Stop being the world's best kept secret and share your gifts with us. We're waiting!

KEY TAKEAWAYS

- One of the best ways to stay on track regardless of whatever life throws your way, is to encapsulate the most important aspects of your brand into one handy little document called your Brand Blueprint.
- You can download your Brand Blueprint template for free at SizzleForce.com/BrandBlueprint
- No one ever changed the world by hiding. It's time for you to get out there and share your greatness so you can make a difference!

ACKNOWLEDGEMENTS

I have wanted to write a book for as long as I can remember. Doing so, is no easy feat. This book is in your hands today because of the love, support and encouragement so many showered upon me.

Special thanks to...

All of my amazing clients. Thank you for trusting me! Thank you for giving me the opportunity to walk along side you as you create your riveting success stories. I'm so excited for each and every one of you!

Amanda Jones, my wing woman, you are an absolute treasure! Your unending love and support mean more than you'll ever know. I'm quite certain you are actually a superhero in disguise. Thank you for always being there and for taking such good care of all of us, all the time.

Karen Askenaze, Laura Nivinskus and Karen Koczwara, thank you for making me feel safe enough to let you read this book before the rest of the world did and for hunting down every grammar, spelling and punctuation error I overlooked.

Marti Daly & Patti Cain-Stanley, you have walked with me through some of the most victorious and most difficult days of my life. Thank you for showing up every Thursday and for always knowing exactly what to say and when to say it.

Allison Maslan, Chris Friend & Giles Fabris, the work we've done together has impacted my life on so many levels. Thank you for always pushing me outside of my comfort zone, for teaching me how to silence my negative mind chatter and for holding my hand when I'm scared—again and again and again.

My prayer warriors, you know who you are. You prayed for me to find the right words when I needed them most. Your prayers fueled my ability to get this out of my head and onto paper. Thank you.

Mom, for always encouraging me to write a book. You knew I could. Your belief in me means more than you know.

Joshee, Sisi and Bean, thank you for cheering mommy on, for celebrating each little accomplishment with me and for understanding when I had to hibernate so I could get this book finished. I love you more than I know how to express.

Kevin, for being you. Because of you, this dream I had of writing a book has come true. You are the most loving, loyal, kind, intelligent, talented, God-fearing man I have ever known. It's a privilege to be your wife. Here's to the rest of our lives!

Jesus, I would be nothing without you. Thank you for loving me even tho…

120

ABOUT THE AUTHOR

Stephanie Nivinskus

Stephanie Nivinskus is the CEO of SizzleForce Marketing, a boutique branding agency that specializes in storytelling. Since 1995 she's been developing brand building campaigns that have been used by Fortune 500 companies including Starbucks, Sprint, The National Football League and Cox Communications along with hundreds of small, privately-owned companies. Stephanie is also the creator of SizzleForce Marketing Academy, a digital training platform for small business owners that want to learn how to master their own marketing. In addition to writing this book, she has written for Forbes and Entrepreneur magazines. Stephanie delivers keynote speeches throughout the United States.

Stephanie has been married to her Mr. Wonderful since 2000. They live in San Diego with their three amazing children and 3 crazy cats.

BOOK STEPHANIE TO SPEAK

Stephanie Nivinskus is a keynote speaker known for captivating audiences with her humor, high energy and ability to break complicated marketing topics down into bite-sized pieces that can be immediately implemented.

Since 1997, Stephanie has been inspiring and equipping corporate executives, consultants and small business owners to get noticed and attract more clients with innovative, heart-centered marketing strategies and tactics.

To watch Stephanie's sizzle reel, read audience reviews, download her speaker sheet or book Stephanie for your next event, visit SizzleForce.com/speaking OR call/text 858-578-9674.

CONNECT WITH STEPHANIE

Website: SizzleForce.com

Email: ClientCare@SizzleForce.com

LinkedIn: LinkedIn.com/in/stephanienivinskus

Facebook: Facebook.com/SizzleForce

YouTube: Tinyurl.com/SizzleForceYouTube

Pinterest: Pinterest.com/SizzleForce

Mailing Address:
10755 Scripps Poway Parkway #134 San Diego, CA 92131

PLEASE SHARE YOUR THOUGHTS!

Did this book stir up some new ideas for you? It would bless me deeply if you would take a few minutes to write a short review on Amazon right now!

I read each and every review (and so do my awesome children)! I'm committed to using your feedback to make this book even more valuable in future editions.

To leave a review right now, visit:
SizzleForce.com/BookReview

Made in the USA
San Bernardino, CA
14 February 2019